YEAR ZERO

Brian Henderson

YEAR ZERO

Brick Books

CANADIAN CATALOGUING IN PUBLICATION DATA

Henderson, Brian
  Year Zero

Poems.
ISBN 0-919626-77-7

I. Title.

PS8565.E5Y4 1995   C811'.54   C95-931299-4
PR9199.3.H46Y4 1995

The support of the Canada Council and the Ontario Arts Council is gratefully acknowledged. The support of the Government of Ontario through the Ministry of Culture, Tourism and Recreation is also gratefully acknowledged.

Cover is after a photograph of a work done by the Nupe people of Nigeria. *Women's Wrapper*, which is part of the Emma Harter Sweetser fund collection, resides in the © Indianapolis Museum of Art. Author photo by Brenda Clews.

Typeset in Trump Mediaeval. Printed and bound by The Porcupine's Quill. The stock is acid-free Zephyr Antique laid.

Brick Books
431 Boler Road, Box 20081
London, Ontario
N6K 4G6

CONTENTS

The Winnowing Horizons

Mother Tongue

THE WINNOWING HORIZONS

... if like a shade
you yield your remains ...
who will shelter you? The road ahead
is not a way; only two hands, a face,
those hands, *that* face, the gestures of one
life that's nothing but itself,
only this sets you down in that Elysium
crowded with soul and voices, in which you live;

and the question you leave behind, that too
is one of your gestures....

– Eugenio Montale

Darkness. The lake
with its language of swallowed things

Sick with distance, they
circle back
as if following a shoreline

They rise from the centre

The air is rich with unfinishedness

Things want to be free
impossibly
without having to be lost

IN THE SICKROOM

(for my Father)

The painted screen that no one owns
puts out blossoms, silk blue
wash of shadow, darker
blue of staves of branches
which afford the warblers
niches to sing from

or dexterous, wings
cerulean, white, grey, afan,
to catch the golden insect
on the knotty bark

Everything appears in bloom here –
the red seed heads of the fruit,
death too, an ornamental rat
on blue ground, gnawing
at white stamens of bone –

hiding the tumbled sickbed,
dark boat that ferries you away
in the pouring window light

KOTO MUSIC, TORONTO

Wave lengths of silk
string, distilled on air
Through the window, stars of bone:
listen

Things so divergent, only our mutual
speed allows us to perceive them at all

The koto still
within earshot, though the music is
floors down

as if I've already lived a life
but cannot twist back to it
through the narrow stairwells
where I am only a guest and
spears of sound go flying

scattering me, scattering into me
the edge of everything
where you've already crossed,
evicted by what held you,
at the edge of glass

of dark water, liquor, opaque with blasts
of mirror I suddenly, and only
for a moment, see some part of myself in

refusing to identify us
or any other precipitous thing

I might say I recognize this voice
but I do not; it comes as if
from under the earth,
encrusted with a fragrance too heavy to bear

It curls up, a nautilus
of cloud in the south west –
a book of backward spiralling
mother-of-pearl blackened light

You have hardly begun the poem
the voice says, and yet
many people have already died

We open even a word like a book
I try to say, but how does this help,
when in the living
every lit vein runs to the golden stigmas of the heart

Perhaps the only real word is
the one the body speaks
as a whole life

and only with our whole lives
can we read it

VALEDICTION

(for bpnichol)

There is all this *talk*, but language
wants you for itself
It wants you to shoot
its colours through, to dye
with its flood:

pearl-grey and mother-of-pearl
rose and yellow and black, powder of iridescence:
wings of butterfly

It wants to give you the kiss of mother
tongue: mute, matrixed, so that what you speak
is a second language you never master

Still you want to have some names

They happen in a zone where you finally
catch up to what's been, all this time,
following you like a law
sleeping in high black stone,
bowls of snow, alpine meadows
something so brilliant
you breathe it like a knife
of ice, of prisms in blasting sun

You are one word
claimed by language

What happens, once you are said?

(for Gwendolyn MacEwen)

Along this river, shore birds cut
hieroglyphs in failing light

Dusk moves with the sweep of a hand

From the mouth of the moon
your shadow glides out,

Egyptian
among discarded languages,
broken tongues, ruins,
robbed tombs, codes of stars,
a shiver over the landscape
that once thought itself green
or perhaps human

Nerve speech spilt out of you
its pleasure sparked along
your limbs, hot tongues, burned
you up like furniture
calls you back to itself
crackling through the night unnoticed
forking out in new directions

and along your body strips of gold unfold

(for Eli Mandel)

YOU SAY the cow is smoking a pipe, and I
believe you. You wave to the stranger
on the other side, and row across
the river to reach her, though there is
no river, no boat. You are
doing all this with words, undressing
the night from her blouse of blazing
stars....
        But I can only imagine
what this world is for: it burns
memories like a wick. They flare up
gutter out. Heat lightning. Words –
you make me say – enact
what they do not mean. Or mean
what they do not signify. Oar.
That river again

The sky has fallen into the arms of the
river, like a lover, but remains still
overhead,
        striking a burst of heat
lightning from her own darkness,
all distance
        collapsed in the expanding
space between

AT PHYL'S FARM, HANOVER, ONTARIO

(for Aunt Phyl)

The sky has nothing to do with this
Death sheds
a dark clarity
upward from the house –
a cloud luminous with distance
gets caught in the wild white pines,
hollyhocks and clematis

Whinnying from the barn
and the storm of flies:
rips in memory that know and forget
Something is torn here
and yet everything is smooth, unblemished

Everything now belongs completely
to her – more so even
than when she could touch it
Her touch no longer needs to lie along things
but takes itself away like a glance ...

the heavy glassware displaying its cuts

LAST DAYS: WATERCOURSE WAY

(for Dick)

The reservoir, no longer reserved,
using up its name in a flood bursts
muddy, supple and fast

The flood floods through you, you are
its course. The river
lies down in you to keep moving

Where were any of us standing
that we thought we could merely be
watchers?
The current burns

Your hand doesn't want these words
waves them aside, you are becoming
a flood plain –
so many broken, speechless and
used up things

burning
through us

FLYING, SOMETIME AFTER THE FUNERAL

(for Dick)

The eyes of the night sky
the thousandfold,

the moon a skinning knife, our shadow

falling from us
hungry for the earth, weightless
heavier than we are

We speed into space
that never exhausts its
deceptive clarity, its
discipline of thresholds, until
perhaps at the last moment
(whatever that is, or is like)

Below, clouds silt up the valleys
whitely, with the amnesia of snow

You have left us, still here, moving
where what refuses to absorb us forever
calls us over and over to its refusal

These mountains: stonewater
The apparition of
an abandoned boat
adrift in the heart of a high lake

Crossbills crisscross the big larch
Rock and ice cresting beyond and below us
are a going down, a going
under, current
in geologic time

This mourning – a cove of blue light,
thrown shadows, dis-
locutions – is double,
ochre and purple, we
two

NORTH SHORE, DOMINICAN REPUBLIC

On the black flotsam of seaweed
a broken conch opens coral whorls

The whole island is coral, ancient,
grottoed, bone white, under
lianas, the hot red bloom of *flamboyance*

The root of the coconut palm
is a skeletal hand on the cart path

There in the field, a hill of skulls
at the point of the eruption of the imaginary
the unreconciled, what trails us
from another country

(for Gramp)

Snow retreats into itself
in the light fall of winter rain
the feeders attract dirty yellow clouds of
raucous grosbeaks. Siskins, purple
finches, juncos flash through the architecture
of trees like memories on the edge of memory,
then are seen clear
in the dim shimmer of wind at the top of
a stairway

The lake a landing of white
holding itself still, brighter than sky,
condenses a line of haze
like a sleeping, or a dying, body over its icy rim,
the weather for the first time in months
above zero

The house glows with what lives leave
behind

(for Dad)

The loon's tricky shakuhachi
cuts us adrift in starwater

Your old name sails by
with a roof of lightning
(Look, look, my childhood
insists on seeing me)

The warp of hills is pulled
into view and lost again
in the looming rain

You were born by the lake
over its depths, bright
as a leaping fish
Now a burning hook
jigs in the reeds of sky

Death passes its tranquil current
beneath us, and swallows our images whole

Hung on the spider's line
a laundry of insects, these words

Blue becomes more and more perfect,
intense as the sun leaves it

Night sky with its stave of stars,
its X-rays, trussed with loss

Not only are the dead living
but the animals are human
out there beyond the wavering lights

The table unfolds its legs like a spider
in the mansion of darkness

But here, in this futile glow,
your helpless wheelchair
stands

I cannot don
a suit of scales or wings or
get the martinis out
we both miss now

What's worse, this sonata of memory
I am custodian of, seems to have no coda
and is nearly impossible to listen to

SHADOW LAKE: STANDING IN STARLIGHT

The starlight stalls here, and almost reaches me –
the sound of something too distant
or too old to cut me out of the background
with listening. Nonetheless it beckons me

I feel it nearing, feel
that it has always been nearing –
this fossil of sky-knowledge

Who beckons it, or sends it on its way?

Scatter of pauses bursts upon me
without movement

while heat lightning shimmers the low blackness
to the south. The memory of it
forgets itself over and over in steep flashes

Water birds wake the echo of a shore
as if from a great distance

What is gone forever, haunts
and ekes itself out through me

Snow ghosts, frozen fish fence
Things dive in the grain of wind
Here, there are many waves of dying

Snow locks its water up in a flake
a star house, its passion for a shape
in the middle of May

Who would not be happy
when the night flies out
like a shaken sheet
its pattern haunted with memory
before there was memory

and you see the wick of
flesh spit its flame
burning the names, the long longing
as they are drawn through

And these are only fuels,
passion of *dis-* and *re-*
shaping, with their burr of beat,
the big drum of earth

I feel like all of Ellesmere island
in February embrace

Your face looks so much younger,
softer, but beyond the disease
rather than before it, melting

You are a
glow in the shroud of white

Lightning wicks the cupola ambergris of clouds,
sky booms off the pitch reaches of itself

I am one of many peripheries

The house once lit with desire and fear
darkens to stone many miles distant

If it's true a house is always dreaming itself,
its rising out of water,
have you come finally to live there?

I chaff you into the lake
the sky also falls into
with its broken ceiling of stars and lightnings
my words blown off course

Loadstone-like, only your name remains
what it defines, gathering
around it, whirlwinding....

There are things I can't seem to speak of
but these things, somehow, will insist
surreptitiously, on speaking for me
recalling me, you to me

window opening in my midst, eye,
white sail in winnowing horizons

THERE IS A KIND OF MUSIC
an unfinished music
to this constantly moving house
an opening and closing of breath
like a tide of shadows

Who would have guessed how much
we depend on listening for it
and on not hearing it

Death is a stagger in the rhythm
so you hear it for the second time
Birth is the first

It flies up like a child's cry
It is the home of blood, of birds
of sooty wing whose songs are hard

We come all this way to lose ourselves finally
and it's family we find ourselves doing it in –
not the father tongue my mother taught me –
but the house in a cradle, another language
an island the music moves
sweeps as if it had hands
and nearly comforts

What's it doing here, this notebook? It's a shadow, a hole in the chipped green coffee table. I want to avoid it. How can I write about you?

The sky with its aluminum shimmer has hidden the sun. There is a glowing surrounded by body. Looking out the window I see a redstart. It flashes from branch to branch, song in its empty throat. The book that was nothing before but space has now, at least, a bird in it. You'd like that Dad, anyway.

But OK, it's not really from out of nothing anything begins. As in the Mayan tribe where spouses are grown, things are watered, pruned, unfurl. They even have ears. Tropical with growth when the warblers return from the south, they draw colour from the blackness of earth. You are this earth. And it begins with memory, with loss. It is what breaks when you name it.

You always wanted to winter elsewhere than in winter, the sky burning with birds and birdsong, clouds of gaily-coloured birds, butterflies, those who have gone to the other side. You wanted to sail the islands.

Here the chestnut displays its floral white towers, the bird's-eye maple its yellow-green tassels, the birch and aspen their cascades of catkins. Along with everything else (these leaves, warbler wings), the wind also reads the spider's book of lungs. In May everything is still being written, even death, disappearance. The annular eclipse, glimpsed through the soft lens of cloud, incinerates the shadow of the moon. I am a thing thrown, cast. A shadow.

* * *

The little notebook collects fear, fretting, sharp shards of grief, until I'm stalled in the middle, neither ending, nor beginning, nor continuing. Stupid! Continuing not continuing, my life a ghost of your dying. What I learn, it seems, is what is taken from me, what I give up. I am being evaporated, exhaled unendingly.

* * *

But you are a lens through which vision moves. The image disperses, moves on, or becomes merely unperceived. Rilke says it's earth wanting to become invisible. Wanting, wanting, how much of that is left behind. You move out now beyond the horizon of the heart, and give us our own hearts back.

* * *

Flung out. I can't really imagine that final flungoutwardness. The Chinese elm spends itself in a storm of seeds that the steep noon sun seems to make clatter with light. You are spilled. Released.

* * *

I wake this morning early, the ground buried, drifted in with a profusion of future, each one almost like the others. Brenda's foot, slipped from under the sheets, seems to want her sleeping self to start on some journey. Perhaps she's already dreaming it.

The night hurls itself past starlight
with such stillness, I scarcely notice
how it keeps leaving the distance of the sky
to come at me, like a voice, or
the space for a voice

Everything else is whispering, following
catching up with me, failed
freer of the bones, caretaker
of the lost, the tossed away

What does it mean to fall, and keep
falling, as if
there were no such thing as ground,
except to be followed
by afterimages?

How could I have loved you more
once our differences remained
unspoken?

Do the real images then precede
the body falling?
Is it you gliding toward me,
the jib of ash in the unfurling wind,

your clarity,
while for us the horizon is always
only approaching?

Thrown off by the night, shooting stars,
burning up the arcs
of their own entrances,
trace the night's speed

A NET, A THROW
of feeling outward, toward
you, who continue
to fly through and on
as if one or the other of us
were imaginary

Trying to retrace this
tracery, calling you,
calling you back
to explain things to me
though I know it's impossible

You lean into my dreams
as if against a membrane

you, who are no longer
happening to yourself
but to me

MOTHER TONGUE

The children were there, they were shadowy figures
outside the fence, indistinct as
distant blobs of faces at twilight.
I can't remember, anymore,
the moment I turned to take them....
                                        I can't
remember the journey from the center of the field to
            the edge
or the cracking of the fence like the breaking down of
            the
borders of the world, or my stepping out of the
ploughed field altogether and
taking them in my arms....

                              – Sharon Olds

LIGHT GLAZES us, and scrawls, flares
over our limbs, hair; there
is something extravagant

about us now, our being
together in this moment of new colour

Nearly translucent
reds, yellows, limes flame
the air, ripe with
bursting them out, their perfumes

loading us with everything
that adheres to us – what we've tried
to forget, tried to recall –

sticking the warblers to their songs

Blackburnian orange and black to faces, the dead

burn through us,
the not yet born

Our bodies an asterisk
of scatter

As in a dream the blue fish
hovers in summer lightning
imagining itself, momentarily a form
of electric energy, perhaps high
above the rain and its mouth of thunder

(it is so humid we too seem to lose our bodies
and find them again in another element –
some half successful journey
in a time machine –

above the amniotic forests
of teal lianas and blood sugars)

and watches from a chronic distance
the flickering immobility
it will deliver me to

BULBS of lungs that do not breathe,
huge saurian head, fierce

with Jurassic time, you rehearse
the archaic, invisible, unseeing

or looking inwards, you are
parasitic in the floating world

you've created, with enzymes
you've dissolved tissues to get bloodfood

The brain glimmers through
translucent skin, the delicate tree of veins

Organs migrate through you
you're imagining
a different order we have already
placed ourselves within
and are busy being changed by

Tail, ribs unfurl, condense to bone
you raise a big head

Who can recognize you, already
remote, already human, your heart
a balloon on a string
oh little one?

SPLASHED BENEATH YOURSELF

with a line of yellow

mirrored in the mica of October water
(a mind embracing another's thought)

your body marks it, comes upon it
by carrying it

Once fish, once larva,
tiny amphibian of the Cambrian
everglades your blood writes, it hides

its face in you, glides
towards the surface of name

is, in a rush of wind, erased
and then calls to itself again
over the deepness that closes beneath it

Your body's unlocked with it, your
body of work, like a gold key, a fragrant
water lily that floats over its millennia
like a roof

Like the lake that holds you
you are a dwelling, with a feast
and a guest, a red door
burning in that lake

A KIND OF TURNING and
recalling, embodiment

The shades drawn, light
is a net in its room,
celebrated at one table

The plate fraught with fruit, fall
branches spending their coin in a sluice of wind

The room is calm water, but
the dead, whose faces still
haunt the walls, the mantels, would cry, would cry out
at my approaching

What has the body meant? Re-
hearsing *Souffles*, breathing, re-
reading, you nourish it, are the point
of turning, though no longer small,

Hecate's place, the place
of cross-roads crossing itself in you
between harsh shadows

a star risk,
this ripening with hormones – a night sky
referring to another writing
outside the night –
floods the violence, the real
hard breathing

FEBRUARY: FLASH POINT

Wind ignites a magnesium of snow, the air
a continuous flash that forgets
everything it once knew

Like weather, you move over within yourself,
an adoration, and disown the
shapes you blow through

You are gestating incandescence
whose shadow shortens
to that telling moment I can tell and
tell, and say nothing of

and strewing the ash of snow, a drift of selves
in the tiny creases of your landscape

you are filled to your season
with others

welcoming us to the eye
of the blizzard

THE HUMMINGBIRD

(for Dad)

Green lanterns of leaves cling
to their lifelines,
ragged with storm light

The lake crashes over
lake-made dykes of the marsh
slewing sand
back over blades of yellow iris

The water maple, undermined like you
by incremental dynamite of surf
topples finally into the wet lap –
a green torch
being thrown, in slow motion, away

I have nothing if not this
forever unravelling shore
that marks the changing
line between water and water
to stand upon now

I'm no longer sure
what direction *forward* represents

Maple fruit torque through the wind,
propellers of future raining down

Your grandchild in his mother's womb, stirs

After the storm a hummingbird
checks out the bright life-
jacket sprawled on the deck, whirs off

SHELLS

(for Brenda)

Honeycomb, skull, seed
silence, a mouth, an ear

in fact you are a room, a
rumour, holding, transforming and transferring
under the roof of blood

You drench our new one with meanings
bestow them as gifts, scatter them
with laughter

You are the thorny oyster
of Quetzalcoatl's house –
the turbine, the winds of storm

or Vishnu's Cabinet, pregnant with words
perfect and contrary (turning away
from time, and in it, in which
after the flood had swept them away,
the god brought the Vedic scripts
back to his people), you scatter

you, the continuer, more-than-one,
unfold your arms and sweep away once again
these gods, stories, heedings and bindings
with your serene embrace

Because with its hot gathering
you are bearing the unbearable

the shape of your kiss
the leafy venus

The first moon is a grinding moon
through the mill of night,
strewing bright bone dust over dark ground

The second moon scratches with diamond point
the unscratchable sky

The third moon waxes a ghost of itself in the dawning,
playing a ghost music: a koto's
quill of sound, arrows and gongs

Your belly is the fourth moon, full of child
approaching its birthing hidden,
and the nearer the more so

The fifth moon is nearly a word
smudged just over the horizon
on the way to a language –
perhaps even the name that calls him forth

The sixth moon will be the fishhook of souls,
the seventh the boat, the tipped cradle

The eighth moon the witch's basket
(heaped with nocturnal herbs)
The ninth the knife running away with the spoon

WHAT IS NAMED, FALLS. Stars
graze our roof, little glitter

of hot star silt floods you, astra
knot, cord, you are
its parachute, its deep,

the field of
what lets the earth fall into itself:
blue nectarines, pink mangos

fierce planets, comets, suns, all
the unspoken and heavenly
bodies of the house of milk

in fact the whole sky
rising out of you
new, nameless, and unfathomable being

EARTH WARD

(for Kyra)

Unfinished, the centre still gathers
to scatter

Bees unzip the tropic of afternoon

and through weaving heat lines
the ear thinks space: worlds
wavering in and out, urth-
ink: hot colours

pushing from inside the seventh month,
August, and I am listening, listening
at the door of your house,
my ear to taut skin

The whirl of the heart, your thinking
beginning now to bud, as I
grow down to wood, to bone

You spill toward your human hearth
with the speed of darkness, a whir
outward, earthward

I fool myself into thinking
I can hear you
readying your shining cry

(for Brenda)

The dream light that folds
through the page and washes over it
as water, is afternoon
light and wells upward

We cease to read, or read more
deeply the deep beneath
the water's face, over which
only reflexions, echoes glide

There is no law in the afternoon

but a nimbus of orange, yellow, red
burning out through the still green
heart of the crab apple

The afternoon expands
its hive of warming air in its
deep scatter of things

shivering, breathing, as if
like honeycombs, the nothing of light
withheld in everything, begins to bloom
with a blaze of wings, a brideflight

up from the folding
the unbroken opening you continue to write in
the feminine plural
who's never yet not you

AUBADE

Your body, still
sleeping

The push of sun over shale
is almost overheard pink

a kind of magma, the pressure
of the almost arrived

Each leaf flourishing in sun-wind
is a small clashed cymbal for it

All along the boundaries, over everything,
you are traversed, suffused, populated
because there's the mother
and then there are all the others

The light along your arm marks it
as an aspect of its own rising depth
remembering itself in you

If the sun pours itself into your ear
do you hear gold?

For breakfast: a pear
the juices spreading down your lip
a cloud of finches
an unfinished sentence

Nor has I written this

IF LANGUAGE IS NOT STRANGE to itself
how can it be its own?

A word is a hunger, a power spot
like a body, a sea

flooding itself with fish, sown
with currents, glimmers

Beyond its margins palms wave

Deep in the ground
it pulls minerals from rocks
and listens to the talk of fossils

is given
gills, feathers, fire, palm fronds
spun with the silk of memory

and when we are re-
membered through its shimmering, alien
depths, we can listen with our skins

The heart that flutters there is
almost heard

overheard

over the wash of sea-pull
womb-beat: the wings

of a hairstreak

JOUR NÉ ONE

(for Brenda)

*

Before,
there was a woman with two hearts
the not yet and the still

Can I remember hearing
both beat together?

*

Your storm breaking so fiercely
around me, soaring with pain

it was all I could do
to remember how to breathe

*

You were opening and closing
glowing transparent, and

to the two who dwelt in the body
the pain said, *One of you must leave*

I had thought it was raining
but there was no outside
everything was darkening and lightning
pouring and brightening

leaving and entering
one and the same

*

It's you, it's you
two-headed woman
opening your mouths and crying the
river of blood that floats
you over the bed, the sky, the
sky blue cord, after the hurricane
you are the tropics and the coast for,
shaken, rapturous, flooding

*

Nothing
is irrevocable
but this

The moment will not collect itself but
shoots through
like a glance, a long look,
everything we know
shoots through this first
meeting, which gives it its
irrevocability, its
scary splendour and permeability
under the glow of vernix

Ecstatic as a cloud
the sun breaks through
your body
he on you looking
eyes on yours

Now nothing is
lost or ever
the same

(for Adrian)

Blossoming out of body
into body, miraculously
human in the ply of night
with a waiting name

You open something in me like a wound

Tulip cry from Brenda's flesh

you pulled a message of blood after you
streaking the bed of night red

I am an envelope of arms
and you the letter whose address
is yourself

garden of delight

You must have come out pondering the future
because your hand was clasped to your cheek,
and then you threw out your cry
following that long series of your mother's,
dragging a parachute of blood
out of her sky
so the bed became a salty red sea
that flowed without seam or stop

She was waxen, pale
with a purple centre
and I thought she would die
when the medic lifted her out
to the raft of the stretcher

Your first night in the world
your mother was accompanied by flashing
lights to the hospital,
while still at home you slept
on my tide-swept chest in
your cocoon of blankets

In the clear cold of morning, we
taxied our way to her,
she who was ripe with milk
and weariness, and she unwrapped you
like a gift, she whose gift you are

A bee's flight
in the naked methane of evening
striking its yellow match

Whatever is the fire
invisibly searing holes in the once-
bluer-than-blue drapes?

It pours its carnal ribbon through you like
wet lightning in a line squall
calling your name out of you like a debt:

the one who fears, the one
who hurts, the one
who screams, the one
who clings, the one
who births, the one
who triumphs, the one

who celebrates the *O* of air
sucked into new wings,
lungs of our new daughter
as she stretches hotly, redly
beside you on our bed

MOONSET

The mouth of some enormous drinking glass
is pouring its liquor of burnt gold
across the ghostly lake just
before dawn

It is the mouth of a sleeping body, agape,
a birth spot, spilling
golden speech, mink skull and gull
wing, sandblasted shard of
beer and champagne bottle,
iridescence of kingfisher
feather, fiery lip
of burst balloon, bleached
wing of vertebrae, hearts' desire,
onto the dream of beach

Flickering on water
like scales of pike, it is
molten glint of the
future, of things, of the
insistence of things, goldenly

And it beckons you to want it
to go on flickering
forever

In the late summer of 1983, my Aunt Phyl died, my father's sister. She'd lived alone with her horses, and was found floating in her pool. She was a year younger than my father.

Dad was ill with a rare disease related to M.S. called Shy-Drager and was being guinea-pigged at North York and Toronto Western. In and out of hospital, he kept losing consciousness, mostly for a split second only, but often enough time for him to collapse. It took them a long time to figure out the problem, and then there was no cure. Slowly he lost other aspects of his life.

My wife and I were married three days before his death, and eleven months after her father, Dick, died of emphysema. He was 63.

In the fall of 1985 my Grandfather died. He was 97 and had outlived my Grandmother by over 20 years. His was a longed-for death.

Then others, associates, acquaintances – like my family, also people from whom I'd learned – passed away, and the manuscript could no longer be (if it ever was) an elegy, or even elegies, but instead cut glass, folding water, streaming wind.

I wanted to dedicate the book, if it ever came to that, to them, but didn't know how to balance the weights of feeling with the form of the dedication as a list of names. And then when the children, Adrian and Kyra, came along and that part of the manuscript started to take shape, it was for them and Brenda, my wife.

Now I felt I couldn't do any dedications. I felt how impossible even multiple dedications were, since the relationships were of such differing textures. They'd all be cracking off in different directions, felt wrong, and would overburden the book, like a tombstone, even though, perhaps even especially because, they are at the heart of it – not their names, but them. And so this is for them.

ACKNOWLEDGEMENTS

The Montale on page 9 is from a translation by William Arrowsmith.

Some of the poems – sometimes in different versions – first appeared in the following magazines: *Descant, Poetry Canada Review, Event, The Antigonish Review, Rubicon,* and in the anthology, *Inside the Poem* edited by W.H. New. I wish to thank the editors. Thanks to Rosemary Sullivan. Thanks also to the articulate sensibilities of Doug Barbour, Doug Jones, and especially to Dennis Lee, whose combined and various insights propelled me to the limits of this book. Special thanks to Don McKay without whom, etc ..., and whose acute sense of image and tone was unflappable even in the face of late revisions.

The Expanding Room
Paracelsus
The Veridical Book of the Silent Planet
Migration of Light
The Alphamiricon
Smoking Mirror
Year Zero

Brian Henderson is the author of seven collections of poetry (including a deck of visual poem-cards) and his work has appeared in a number of small magazines over the years. In the seventies he was a founding editor of RUNE. He has worked in educational publishing for the last decade, most recently as the publisher at Oxford University Press, and now does consulting. He lives in Toronto with his writer-painter wife, two young kids, a small black cat, and some African rift lake cichlids.